# The Pros and Cons
# of Index Annuities

## LINDAHL LUCAS

# TABLE OF CONTENTS

# Introduction

Surely you have turned on the television or computer and seen many ads directed to retirement. You may feel they are directed at you, and they are. Today, there are so many people and companies trying to sell, drive or push you in a certain direction as you are trying to prepare for your retirement. What is best? Only you can make the choice.

Getting the right information can be hard at times because you might feel that all you are given is propaganda to make you think or feel a certain way, or invest in something you may or may not want. This book is focused on the benefits and negatives of annuities with a complete overview of all types of annuities to help you understand what an annuity is and if an annuity would be a good or bad choice. Pro or con, you can make the right choice.

I believe that I had all of the same questions that you do:

- Why should I buy an annuity?
- Is it a wise fit for me?
- How do they work?
- What is a worst-case scenario?
- Why is an annuity a wise investment for my retirement?
- Which package is the best one to choose?
- What are the differences between index and variable annuities?
- What are the pros and cons of annuities?

Can you think back to when you were young and loved riding a roller coaster? When I think back to my first visit to Disneyland and the sensations that I had riding a roller coaster, they were exhilarating. Many of us can relate to the fact that roller coasters are for the theme park and it is not as enjoyable riding the ups and downs in your retirement. When it comes to your retirement portfolio, to real life and dealing with your retirement, there is no place for sharp ups and downs. They can turn a picture perfect retirement into an extremely challenging disaster. No one wants their hard-earned savings or retirement riding the proverbial roller coaster where there are more downs than ups. What I expect that you want is more and more protected ups and avoiding the downs in a safe and secure way?

As you read each chapter in "The Pros & Cons of Index Annuities" you will find I have based all the conclusions in this book on statistics, research and information gathered, coupled with my years of experience as a licensed insurance agent. I am pleased to share what I have learned with you and this next fact is a shocker to most, I must admit.

You may be surprised to learn that the number one fear of all retirees is running out of money. Ninety three percent of all retirees fear that more than death itself. According to AARP, 10,000 people are turning 65 each day in the U.S. and will be doing so for the next 20 years. How do you think that will affect Social Security, Medicare and even state and federal pensions when you are living in retirement?

Honestly, no one can predict the future, and after spending the time doing the research to write both this book and my first book "Retirement Reality Check," frankly I am scared. The old ways that people like you and me were raised to think about our retirement and our future as we're getting older—those days are gone. What were once the golden years of retirement no longer exist on the same terms as we were taught years ago.

Being prepared for your retirement is an

important task that often needs attention long before you are behind the eight ball. You realize you need a safe place that will protect your money from loss and inflation, and at the same time allow it to grow at a reasonable rate to continue generating you a nice retirement income. This book will make understanding index annuities simple and our goal is to provide you with this complementary information to help you succeed.

There are quite a few choices and options for investing in your retirement and choosing one that is best for you is extremely important. Many professionals may advise that they have the answers for your savings, retirement fund or assets. Most of these people will advise you to invest into the stock market or real estate. Both are very risky investments if you're not protected by an index annuity.

Many of the wealthiest and most financially savvy people recommend or have their assets invested in index annuities. Ben Bernanke, Former Chairman of the Federal Reserve has two annuities which represent the largest percentage of his own personal investment holdings. Ed Slott, who advises thousands of people all over the U.S. regarding their retirement. Individuals such as, Tony Robbins, who describes the financial benefits of index annuities in his book "Money-Master the Game." We should learn from the wealthy and the wisest economists that lead by example, where they know their money is well protected and earning real significant growth.

For the last century, we have been taught to follow the status quo. We have been taught that if we follow the rules, we would be rewarded. However, anyone who has lost money in the stock market knows how shallow that promise really is.

A far better choice for investing in your retirement is to have insurance that can protect your gains and your principal investment. That is what fixed index annuities can do. Annuity policies completely protect an individual against the risk of losing their hard-earned assets. When you invest with us in an index annuity, you are covered by licensed insurance companies similar to a common insurance policy you would have for your home, auto or health protection.

There are two types of fixed annuities: indexed annuities and traditional annuities. Both types are regulated by the government or government insurance departments and then sold via different insurance agents, banks or other registered representatives.

An indexed annuity, like any insurance policy, is a contract between an insurance company and you. At the basic level an index annuity is a tax-deferred investment vehicle that is insured against any loss. Your index annuity is linked to an equity index, usually the Standard and Poor's (S&P 500) or other international indexes.

The index annuity also offers a guaranteed income account value (IAV = pension account value) rate of interest ranging from 3% to as high as 8% compound or simple interest growth.

During the buildup period is when you make either a hefty payment or a sequence of payments, and the insurance company credits you with a return, which is based on changes in the securities index. After the buildup period, you can withdraw income as you need it or turn the IAV into a pension and the insurance company will make guaranteed payments to you under the terms of your contract for the rest of your life and your spouse's life. Then, of course, you may always opt for receiving your contract value in lump sum or continue receiving the annual disbursements based on your policy terms.

The index crediting strategy works as follows: Assuming an index annuity established on the S&P 500, which makes 10% one year, the terms you agreed upon state the fees will be 2.5% and the return on an uncapped investment strategy will be 10%.

Introduction

In such a scenario, you would only receive 7.5% (10%-2.5%) return from your annuity. Some index annuities have caps on the growth of the account. Together, our firm and I review that information with you or your agent to assist you in making the best choice.

An indexed annuity contract is appropriate as part of the asset portfolio for those who want to minimize risk and are either retired or nearing retirement age. The purpose behind purchasing an indexed annuity is to obtain greater long-term gains, rather than those provided by low-return vehicles such as money markets, CDs, bonds or mutual funds with higher fees.

The workings of indexed annuities are usually very intricate and complex. Therefore, the returns maximum varies, often depending on the month and year in which the annuity is purchased. As with many other types of annuities, indexed annuities also carry a surrender charge for early withdrawals. The surrender period ranges from three to twenty years. This is also one of the main criticisms of indexed annuities. Today's fixed index annuities have much more liquidity than the old traditional annuities that get the bad rap in the market. A surrender period requires paying a small fee if you want to take more than the 10% of your account in any one year.

This fee is reduced each year usually by 1% until it disappears at the end of the contract.

Although annuities or contract owners have the right to withdraw 10% of the value of the annuity each year, the primary purpose of indexed annuities is to use as retirement savings and pension, as opposed to short-term savings. More and more annuitants successfully use this investment option for short-term needs. Along with protection against losses, tax deferred growth and liquidity with withdrawal of 10% of annuity value permissible annually. This option could provide sources of funding available for emergencies at all times.

## CHAPTER ONE
## Annuities – What is it?

As discussed in the Introduction, an Annuity is an insurance policy, which is basically a contract signed between you (insured) and a company promising you compensation (insurer)

in the event of some future possible losses in exchange for a periodic payment made to the insurer or company.

**http://ProsAndConsOfAnnuities.com/chart**

It is a very straightforward concept: You place or transfer an amount of money to get some protection against a stock market crash or any future incident of huge proportions. Annuities were designed to protect the financial well-being of a particular individual or individuals, for example, in case your 401K retirement savings were cut in half in a stock market crash. This can be avoided from the loss side of things.

There are various types of annuity policies which you can choose from. Some of the different types of annuities policies along with their characteristics are listed below. These are the most common insurance policies around the world, some of which we do not recommend.

- **SPIA—Single Premium Index Annuity:** A one-time lump sum payment that immediately creates a guaranteed annual lifetime payment/income (pension).

- **Traditional Annuities:** This type of

2

annuity is limited and prevents you from access to your investment during the term of the policy. It was created to offer an income stream similar to a pension. Such annuities no longer exist. Ultimately we would not recommend them.

- **Fixed Index Annuities:** An investment and retirement strategy that provides flexibility with access to market growth and liquidity. Can offer an income stream from your qualified and non-qualified assets to you and your spouse for the rest of your lives. We prefer these types of annuities over most other options.

- **Variable Annuities:** An investment and retirement vehicle that uses your qualified and non-qualified assets, generally it is very high in fees and the account can lose value or suffer a complete loss of assets. This type of annuity offers an income stream for you and your spouse for the rest of your lives.

As mentioned earlier, insurance is a method of managing certain risks in life. When you provide insurance companies with qualified and non-qualified assets, the companies invest these assets securely so they grow, and in case of stock market and economic risk they give you a 100% asset protection guarantee. These guarantees are limited to fixed annuity investment vehicles only. I will explain in detail as we move forward in the book. People usually choose an annuity based on their needs and plans to protect themselves in case of any unexpected and incident or tragedy.

Insurance policies date back almost 4,000 years, when the merchants in Babylon sought to protect their commodities during their journeys and transit from bad weather and robbers. Insurance policies as we know them today were actually fashioned in a coffee shop and are attributed to Lloyd's of London in the year 1688. Annuities on the other hand also date back to the Roman Empire where income was paid to an individual or his/her family periodically. However, indexed annuities and variable annuities as we know them today have only existed for a couple of decades.

The annuities of today are basically by-products of insurance policies, so they are usually offered by certified insurance companies exactly like other insurance policies. Originally, annuities were created to protect an individual against the risk of them outliving their income. Annuities are simply the reverse of a life insurance policy. Today with the creation of the fixed index annuity, you have more control, liquidity and benefits than ever before. That is just one reason why we like some annuities.

While a life insurance policy is meant to pay the insured after his/her death (in which case, the money usually goes to his/her family or any other beneficiary), annuities today provide asset growth and protection which can be annuitized (turned into a pension) to pay individuals an annual income for the rest of their lives, no matter how long they live or if their assets get depleted. The current trend is to make annuities a retirement plan, which provides an avenue to save up for retirement. All annuity policies consist of three distinct sections or phases:

1. **Accumulation:** Always the first part in any annuity policy, this is the growth period, which starts after the preliminary payment is made. An individual continues to make periodic extra payments into the annuity policy during the accumulation time.

2. **Annuitization:** This phase describes the point in the policy when the insurance company is required to begin making income payments back to the annuity policy account.

3. **Payout:** This is the concluding phase of the policy in which payments are made to the investor for their lifetime or over a period determined by the contract or the annuity policy.

You can fund your annuity policy in either one or a mixture of the following ways:

- **Single Premium**: One complete lump-sum amount will completely fund the policy. This is common with an IRA or 401K rollovers.

- **Fixed Premium**: Under a fixed premium,

you need to make a fixed payment at regular intervals, for example, $1,000 every month for two years or until the policy is completely funded.

- **Flexible Premium**: Under this type of premium, a minimum amount of premium is set after which you can fund money into your policy whenever and however you choose.

- **Straight Life:** If you choose this method, the company will pay you as long as you live regardless if the policy's value has been exhausted. If your amount has not been exhausted before you die, the remaining amount goes to your chosen beneficiaries.

- **Cash Refund Annuity:** Under this, you receive payments throughout your life, and if there is any principal remaining in your account when you die, it goes to a beneficiary. This benefit of today's index annuity products is met with great enthusiasm by most investors. This is truly a way to pass on your legacy.

- **Period Certain:** With this, you get paid a certain amount whether you live or not.

For example, if your period certain is 25 years and you die after 15 years, your beneficiary will receive the amount for the remaining 10 years. This is not an option that is commonly chosen today.

- **Joint Life:** This is exactly like straight life but instead of one annuitant, there are two, for example a husband and a wife. If one dies the other will receive the payments for the remaining period of the policy, unless the wife dies as well, in which case the payments are made to a beneficiary. This is a most popular option today as it guarantees income for husband and wife for life.

When it comes to timing an annuity policy, you have a couple of options:

1. **Immediate Annuities:** There is no accumulation phase, so these policies begin by making immediate payments

as soon as you fund the annuity and the contract begins.

**2. Deferred Annuities:** Under this option, your initial amount keeps growing until a set time after which the payouts begin. You can choose when the payments begin according to the contract anniversary date.

A critical question is how annuity policies differ from insurance policies.

First, annuity policies can only be really compared with life insurance policies or income protection/disability insurance policies. Annuity policies protect an individual against the risk of outliving their income. So once an individual buys an annuity policy they can choose to leave assets in the account and draw assets as they choose. Or, after a certain time, the individual may start receiving periodic payments, either monthly, quarterly or annually, during his or her lifetime.

Depending on the policy and the state in which that policy is written, an income protection/disability insurance policy it can offer financial support if the occurrence, illness or the disability of the insured becomes incapable of work.

The policy gives monthly support while a life insurance policy provides financial compensation to a decedent's family or any other chosen receiver after the death of the insured, the value of the policy. For this reason, annuities are generally considered reversals of life insurance policies, providing a guaranteed lifetime income.

This does not mean that one is better than the other. Annuities are useful financial products. They all have their unique benefits depending on one's situation and goals.

Indexed annuities are a great option as a retirement vehicle, especially considering the fact that most government and private pension plans use annuities to fund their pensions. It really depends from person to person. Which one best fits your needs. If you want your family to be looked after, if you die, you don't need an annuity policy. You should consider life insurance in such a case.

On the other hand, if you want to save up for retirement and ensure that you and your wife have a secure income for retirement, or some other family member is looked after once you die, you can choose an annuity policy with for example, a joint life, which is the only option still continuously promoted and marketed. You don't have to choose only one of these. You can, for instance, carry a life insurance policy along with an annuity policy as well, both working hand-in-hand for you.

Annuity polices are very important and useful for making life easier and worry-free. They are inexpensive for yourself and your family members. Choosing the right retirement vehicle that allows you to stay protected while still allowing you to participate in gains in the stock market.

Making yourself equitable towards an increase in the market so that you can see reasonable to significant growth in your Index annuity is a great idea. That is why we suggest you complete the questionnaire at:

**http://ProsAndConsOfAnnuities.com/protect**

There you will gain powerful insights on how an annuity policy works.

# CHAPTER TWO
## Indexed Annuity

An indexed annuity is an annuity policy with a twist. Just as there are different insurance policies, you also have different annuity policies to choose from. Annuity policies, also known as fixed index annuities, are a type of insurance policy, which guarantees a full return on the principal amount invested along with a fixed rate of interest on the principal. These policies were intended to work very much like mutual funds but with the added benefit that they are protected from downside risk that can come in the event of a stock market crash. The only difference between the two is that fixed annuities grow completely tax-deferred, which is ideal.

Fixed index annuities function to protect

the principal asset and an individual against the risk of outliving their income. Just like an insurance policy, annuities also create a binding contract between you (annuitant/policy holder) and the insurance company (insurer). With fixed index annuities, the company funds fixed-dollar compensation to the annuitant for the period of the contract, which is usually until the annuitant passes away. This is not the only option. Today, fixed index annuities offer a lot more control. After the contract period is over, you can take your account value and invest it elsewhere, you can set it up to annuitize for a lifetime income source, or you can simply let it grow in the index and be safe with complete access to the asset without penalty. By choosing a fixed index annuity your retirement savings can remain safe and well protected against the risk of loss in the index.

As mentioned in the previous chapter, you can also choose joint life, so your compensation can be paid out to the annuitant as income, and in the event of a death, it is given to the joint owner of the policy, and at the death of the joint owner, it is awarded to a beneficiary. With fixed annuities, the company will offer security for both the principal and the earnings made on the principal. Certified insurance companies usually sell fixed annuities and they have agents and brokers on behalf of insurance companies also sell them.

Within fixed annuities, there are two main branches of annuity polices. The first is commonly known as traditional annuities. These are often regulated by the government or different government insurance departments. They are then sold by means of different insurance agents, brokers, banks or other registered representatives of the government. As with all traditional annuities, the interest paid on the premiums or the principal amount given to the company is set at a rate declared by the company itself.

Many insurance companies that offer traditional annuities are set up and approved through each state's Department of Insurance. The valuable aspect about traditional annuities is that the rate of interest can never be less than the minimum rate quoted in the policy. Although we never recommend traditional annuities for our clients, annuity polices are a good conventional, predictable, secure, money-saving avenue for retirement. Especially if you are incapable of saving because of various reasons, for example, being unable to budget your savings correctly. Annuity rates are typically fashioned from a collection of U.S. treasuries or complementary low-risk, fixed-income mechanisms.

Indexed annuity polices, on the other hand, are always linked to an equity index, either the Standard & Poor's 500 (S&P 500) or other international indexes, for example, the DOW. Indexed annuities also guarantee a minimum interest rate, which usually ranges anywhere from 3% to as high as 7% compounded, or 8% simple. This minimum rate is accurate for most of the indexed annuity policies, but not all policies set a minimum rate. Most of these rate guarantees are part of a rider, called the Lifetime Income Benefit Rider (LIBR) that can be chosen by the client to guarantee a certain interest rate no matter if the index is up or down. This rider is a popular choice with today's retirees.

This is how an indexed annuity policy works. During an initial buildup period, also known as the accumulation period, the annuitant makes a hefty payment or a periodic sequence of payments as discussed in the previous chapter. Next, the insurance company credits these payments with a return based on changes within the securities index in the actual **Account Value**. This depends on the index chosen on your policy. If they chose the **Income Account Value** rider (often called **LIBR**) the annuitant also has an option of interest guarantee. He can choose to use either **Account Value** or the **Income**

**Account Value** (index or LIBR) whichever is higher as a base for income payments. Of course the higher the better and the more you receive in income.

After this phase of the policy, the insurance company will make guaranteed annual periodic payments to you depending on the terms of your policy. You can also choose to receive your policy value in a lump sum later or you can leave the money in the account and draw against it without any penalty throughout your retirement.

Download the worksheet:
**http://www.ProsAndConsOfAnnuities.com/worksheet**

An indexed annuity policy is perfect for people who want to keep their asset portfolios away from the risk of zero income and are already retired or nearing retirement age. The purpose behind purchasing an index annuity is to understand the greater long-term gains of indexed annuities over other financial products.

An indexed annuity policy provides the annuitant with higher potential interest rates unlike the traditional or fixed annuities, because it takes into account the working of an outside stock market index, as stated above, to determine the rate.

This pays interest at a rate derived via a

formula that considers an increase within the outside index, which is subject to a "cap," "spread," and "participation rate."

*The advantage here is that all index annuities have a base of zero which means that in the worst case scenario, the annuitant might not receive any interest on his premiums in that particular year and his assets are always protected and safe.*

The "participation rate" is a percentage set from before and then multiplied by a percentage increase within the outside index.

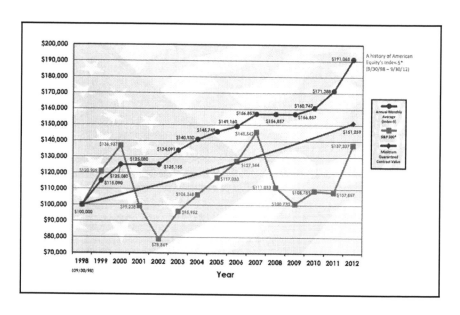

Participation rates, along with caps and spreads, are put into place by the insurance company itself at the start of the annuity policy.

For example, if an index method offers a 50% participation rate, and the return for one particular year was 10%, then the rate would be 5% (10% x 50% participation = 5% return).

A "cap" is a maximum percentage set based on the working of the outside index. For example, if an index method offers 6% cap, and the return was 10% for that year, it would receive a rate of 6%.

A "spread" is a percentage of decrease between the return and the rate the consumer will be credited with. If an index method proposes a 2.5% spread, and the return was 10% for that year, the rate earned would be 7.5% (10% return—2.5% spread = 7.5% return).

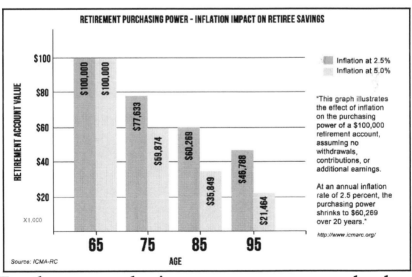

Furthermore, the insurance company also has

the capacity to regulate participation rates, caps, and spreads, also known as "moving parts." The majority of the annuities bought these days have only one moving part, which determines the calculation for the index.

That means an annuity policy could possibly have either a cap, spread or a participation rate. However, some policies combine some moving parts; for example, you can have a cap along with a participation rate in one policy. This does not mean an annuity policy with two moving parts is necessarily a better choice. There is obviously no way of knowing what will occur in an upcoming year. Since the participation rate, spread and cap are undetermined until futures have passed, the best rate or the best performance returns given to your annuity policy are decided based on the annual contract date.

The annual contract date will be set as the date of the contract inception or the date you started the annuity. If you bought a policy on Sept. 1, which will be the official calendar year annual start date, and the index performance will be based on that date. The asset and principal gains are locked in annually and will never be less than the locked in value. A product currently available incorporates an uncapped strategy and includes a spread of about 2%-3.9%, indexed to any one of the various indices. Those investing in index annuities need to select the method of establishing any increase in the index they choose for their policy. The three most regular methods are "annual point-to-point," "monthly average" and "monthly sum," which is also normally referred to in the annuity industry as "monthly point-to-point."

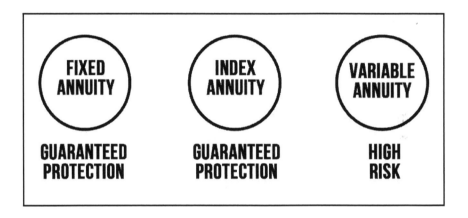

The annual point-to-point method decides the value of the index on the issue date of the annuity policy and balances it to the value of that index on a date in the future, to find out the calculated return on your investments.

The monthly average technique looks at the value of the index on the issue date, and then on each monthly anniversary all the way through the year. The monthly index values are then averaged and later judged against the initial index value, to get the calculated return.

The monthly sum interest crediting system

tracks each month (caps each month), and the outcome from each month is then added up to get the yearly interest rate. With indexed annuities, policy years are not calculated on a calendar year basis but from the day the insurance company invests your premium. The interest is only credited to the policy once a year based on the indexed crediting system.

In addition, once the interest is credited it cannot be taken away during the next year, even if the calculated index is negative. This facet of the indexed annuity is known as "annual reset," which gives a second benefit apart from safeguarding the principal and the following interest gains. It further averts the annuity policy from having to pull through any type of loss to the outside stock index during the past year. For example, if the S&P 500 index dropped to 40% in a policy year, the annuity would be recognized as having no interest for that year.

However, if the S&P 500 had a return of 10% the subsequent year using a yearly point-to-point estimate with a 6% cap, the annuity policy would earn 6% more than the previous year. An illustration of this advantage can be noticed in this example which ignores dividends: with a direct investment in an index with a preliminary investment of $100,000, a 40% loss after one year brings the value to $60,000, and a 10% gain in the subsequent year will augment the value to $66,000.

Learn more at:
**http://www.ProsAndConsOfAnnuities.com/anwsers**

If the same investment were followed in an index annuity policy with an initial investment of $100,000, a 40% loss after one year would be substituted with a 0 and the account balance will still be $100,000. The following 10% gain during the subsequent year is reduced to 6% due to the cap, which would be a $6,000 increase, so the $100,000 investment would then be worth $106,000.

This example demonstrates why annuities

tend to be marketed more seriously towards retirees and seniors, because an indexed annuity policy provides a factual safeguard against market losses and at the same time offers a level of coverage to market based returns. Each of the traditional, fixed and indexed annuities include surrender charges. These charges fluctuate from 20% down to 1% and the policies have surrender charge periods ranging from 1 to 20 years. Usually, the length of a surrender charge period on indexed annuities is from ten to thirteen years. Some annuity policies calculate the surrender charge period from the date the policy goes into effect, while others relate the surrender charge period to each premium paid into the annuity policy that you have purchased.

Traditional, fixed and indexed annuities are retirement savings resources and cannot be used for short-term savings. Today almost all indexed annuity policies offer a penalty-free sum which can be withdrawn every year. You may also give up the surrender charges if the policy is annuitized, which means when the policy is converted into an instantaneous annual income paid over a lifetime. This is usually chosen by the policyholder. Most annuity policies also offer additional clauses to have the surrender charge period waived. This can be done at no extra cost. However, this is usually allowed when the annuitant is either restricted to a nursing home or being diagnosed with a terminal illness, depending on the annuity and the state in which it is purchased. As with all index annuities, money can be taken out from the annuity policy at any time. In most cases up to 10% annually with no penalty on withdrawals. Such an extraction above 10% can be subject to some surrender charges, especially if the annuity policy is still within the surrender charge period and the penalty-free withdrawal has already been used. Annuitants can also choose to receive a disbursement based on the value of the policy for their lifetime or withdraw up to 10% per year.

With an index annuity your assets (qualified or non-qualified) are protected and there is a decreasing penalty for a certain period, and if more than 10% is touched you may be further penalized. Although the penalty declines each year over the surrender period, these annuity policies are not recommended for those with current cash needs and for younger people. Because the money carries some limited liquidity for the contract period, it is perfect for those people who are planning to save for retirement or even those individuals who find it hard to save. To keep the money protected, with limited access only after a certain period of time. Or if desired you have the option to turn on the LIBR and receive guaranteed annual periodic payments either monthly, quarterly or annually during your lifetime. Additionally you could leave the money in the account and use the assets as you choose with guaranteed protection and no withdrawal penalty.

Since this retirement investment vehicle is different from everyday insurance plans, annuities are actually quite beneficial. With insurance plans, the company usually promises to take care of you if you either die, or, for example are paralyzed and unable to work or some other injury takes place. Life insurance protects your spouse and dependents in the unfortunate event that you die or become disabled. You can couple that benefit with the indexed annuity option to establish a source of ongoing income and an end-of-life benefit for your spouse or other beneficiaries. Today's annuities allow you to use the annuity as a tax-deferred investment vehicle with 100% principal and gains protection. Coupling an annuity with an insurance plan can help you live a worry-free life.

## CHAPTER THREE
## Pros and Cons of Index Annuities

**PROS**

A by-product of insurance policies, indexed annuities are products especially for those trying to save for retirement. Insurance companies sell this by-product. The traditional annuity policy gives finance on a set rate of interest while the indexed annuity is intended to pay a fraction of the yearly return on a stock market index, which is calculated on the basis of the Standard and Poor's 500 (S&P 500) or other indexes. The index annuity allows your money to work for you, because of the guarantee. Indexed annuities are sold by licensed life insurance agents and by registered investment advisors.

A great advantage of indexed annuity polices are that they provide the annuitant (person who buys the policy from the insurance company) with higher potential interest rates, unlike traditional annuities. Indexed annuities take into account the working of an outside stock index, for example, the S&P 500 and international indexes as stated above, to determine the rate. The stock market is widely considered the best asset class for continuing growth. An indexed annuity promises to pay a portion of that growth, and in later years the interest on this type of annuity could be very attractive and beneficial.

Indexed annuities pay interest at a rate derived via a formula that considers an increase within the outside index, which is subject to a "cap," "spread," and "participation rate" as discussed.

Index annuities have a base of zero, meaning in a worst case scenario on an annual basis, if an annuitant did not receive interest on the premiums (due to a down year measured in the index performance) the annuitant is still paid the guaranteed interest as was promised at the inception of the annuity policy. What this means can be illustrated by an example. Presume that an annuity will pay 2/3 of the yearly return of the S&P 500. If the index goes up to 30% during the year, then the index account worth will increase by 20% (2/3 of 30 equals 20%) and if the stock market goes down, the value of the annuity will not go down. Instead, the policyholder or annuitant would earn the definite minimum interest rate listed in the annuity policy.

Here is another simple example that may further illustrate an indexed annuity. Let's start with two investment options for $20,000. Option A is investing in a mutual fund indexed to the S&P 500, while Option B is investing in an uncapped indexed annuity tracking the same benchmark, the S&P 500. In year one, the S&P 500 goes down 25%. The resulting value of investment Option A is $15,000. Meanwhile, the value of Option B is still $20,000 due to its downside protection, and it simply adds 0 as interest for that year. The following year, when the index returns 20%, Option A is worth $18,000, meanwhile, Option B is worth $24,000. The protection is a nice to have in a scenario like that.

Another edge gained by investing in index annuities is a mortality credit. The mortality credit is the threshold return on investment that you need for beating the income you get from an annuity, as stated by Moshe Milevsky, an Associate Professor of Finance at the Schulich School of Business at York University. The mortality credit increases significantly as it grows each year on the policy. More importantly, the mortality credit hedges longevity risk, so that you cannot outlive your retirement income. Having the benefit of a mortality credit built into the terms of the annuity often creates a return for scheduled annual disbursement that would be impossible to exist in nearly any other type of retirement investment vehicle.

- **Limited illiquidity helps in saving up for retirement:** The deposit investment or investments made into the annuity policy are secured for a duration of time. With limited liquidity there are surrender charges, often for 10 years or more, therefore an annuity is not a recommended investment for people with the need for financial liquidity or younger individuals.

- **Downside is always protected:** Potential gains are connected to an index option, if the market goes down and no gains are made, then you will not lose any money. For example, a direct investment in an index with a preliminary investment $100,000: a 40% loss after one year cuts the value to $60,000, and a 10% gain in the subsequent year will boost the value to $66,000.

  The same investment pursued with an index annuity policy and with an initial investment of $100,000: a 40% loss after one year is substituted with a 0 and the account balance will still be $100,000. The following 10% gain during the subsequent year is reduced to 6% due to the cap, which would be a $6,000 increase, so the $100,000 investment would then be worth $106,000.

- **Gains are protected:** This is a very attractive characteristic of indexed annuities. If you do make gains from your index option, that gain or profit is protected permanently and your gains never go below that certain amount. To be clear, the upside profits are curbed, no matter what the agent or insurance company tells you.

- **Opportunity to minimize market plunges**: For example, presume the S&P 500 index drops from 1,300 to 900 in one year. Your index for that year will not get any gains, but your next index option will start at 900 on the S&P 500 the following year.

- **Higher payouts for income**: Almost all indexed annuity policies, if and when used for life-span income reasons, have a higher percentage payout than other annuities structured in the same way, for example, variable annuities.

- **Initial bonuses**: This is a great enticement and is offered upfront to do business with the seller. The annuitant will own this bonus in its entirety without issues so long as the covenants of the contract are fulfilled. However, if you cancel your investment early, you only get what you invested; otherwise you start earning interest on the bonus immediately.

Both traditional annuities and indexed annuities authorize any earnings to grow tax deferred until and unless the money is withdrawn in retirement. This tax deferral or suspension allows the annuity's value to grow much more rapidly. The money does not have to be taken out to pay taxes on the gains. Unlike an IRA, there is no limit on how much money can be invested in an annuity to attain tax-deferred earnings.

The idea behind this tax-deferral in an indexed annuity policy is that the financial credit value will grow larger in the annuity compared with the growth in a comparable taxable investment.

An important question here is, why can't you just invest in an IRA rather than an annuity policy? Both provide an opportunity to grow money on a tax-deferred basis. The main reason why you should choose an indexed annuity policy over an IRA is clear.

If you opt for the fixed index annuity that is also known as an equity indexed annuity, you get a complete guarantee of the principal amount. Unlike the majority of mutual funds or securities where the balance of your account continues fluctuating due to the market's performance, the premium deposited in your fixed index annuity cannot go down even if there is a downturn in the market.

That is the primary reason to invest in fixed index annuities.

An Individual Retirement Account (IRA) is in essence an individual savings account with tax benefits. When you open an IRA, it can only be for you, by definition. Therefore, if you have a spouse, you will need to open separate accounts. Unlike indexed annuities, an IRA is not an investment itself. To be more precise, it is an account where you can keep investments such as stocks, bonds and mutual funds. On the other hand, annuity policies along with indexed annuities are insurance products that provide a monthly, quarterly, yearly or lump sum amount of income when you retire. It makes periodic payments for a certain amount of time or until a specific event takes place, usually the death of the person who gets the payments.

Unlike an IRA account, which can only have one owner, an annuity policy can be jointly owned. IRA's also have yearly contribution limits and income restrictions that annuities don't have. In 2014, the maximum an individual could pay into their IRA account was $5,500, or, $6,500 for those 50 years and older. With a single premium annuity policy, an individual is able to fund it all at once. Which is known with any annuity policy, an individual also has the option of naming a beneficiary for the annuity, with various options, for payouts to the beneficiary after the individual dies.

Another huge advantage of indexed annuities, mainly the fixed ones; is the guaranteed stream of income they offer. You have many annuity plans to choose from and once you select one, you receive a certain amount of money on a regular basis. With the nonqualified options on index annuities, a part of every annuity payment shows a return of the premium which isn't taxed. This reduces the amount of income tax levied on your regular annuity payments.

Let's not forget all the other benefits of an annuity; annuities are used today to roll over qualified accounts like IRAs, 401Ks, 403b, TSA-defined compensation plans, Pension accounts and other brokerage accounts. The use of the annuity to protect your assets and to also offer huge upside potential is an amazing fact. A majority of the retired or soon-to-be retired investors are learning to invest in annuities to fund their retirement.

**The different types of payout options an individual can choose from include:**
- **Straight life:** A set dollar quantity, which pays out over the rest of an individual's life, even if the total

payments exceed the amount of original premiums and growth. The disadvantage of this payment option is that the payments will stop at death, even if the total payout is less than the value of your original investment.

- **Joint life:** This choice is for you and a co-beneficiary. If you choose this option, you will be paid as long as one of the two of you is living.

- **Systematic withdrawal:** A set dollar amount or percentage of the contract value paid out yearly.

- **Lump sum:** One single payment which clears up the contribution, letting you take all of the money in cash or move it over into another annuity policy contract.

- **Active participation:** Today's annuities allow you to continue the annuity as a tax deferred investment vehicle with 100% principal and gains protection. This is like a mutual fund without fees, tax-deferred and with protection, resulting in less risk.

If we look at immediate annuities, which as the name implies are instant annuities, the insurance policy or index annuity will start to pay out right away. They are often used by people already retired. Advocates of immediate annuities claim that out of all the fixed index annuities, these are the most useful, especially for those who will not be retiring with a significant flow of pension income. Immediate annuities purposefully use both the interest and the principal amount to create a steady income flow. Moreover, the individual allocations are expected to be higher than anyone could rationalize taking from a balanced portfolio of investments, where protection of the principal balance is usually the main objective of the annuity.

Today you have both the option of a guaranteed fixed rate of as much as 7% to 8% in the retirement account and you have the actual account value that grows with the index. At the end of the day, the annuitant can take whichever account is higher and get an income for life/retirement income or take the full Index account value and do whatever she or he wants to do with it.

Indexed annuities have mostly been devised to include an option to withdraw funds from the annuity annually, so it can be marketed to people from all demographics.

An indexed annuity is analogous to a fixed or adjustable mortgage rate when one buys a new house. An adjustable mortgage rate can be very risky, while fixed-rate mortgage rates vary a lot and are very high.

Annuities pose the same problem. Traditionally, older variations of annuities offered extremely low rates of return while variable annuities are highly volatile, unlike mortgages, a third option does exist offering a middle way with annuities.

The alternative to older traditional annuities and variable annuities happens to be indexed annuities, which provide a median between the other two annuities. This is the best of both annuities' products, and the best investment vehicle currently available for retirement savings today.

Moreover an indexed annuity policy offers a sort of two-in-one policy. Compared to a life insurance policy, which basically compensates you after you die, an indexed annuity policy compensates you while you are alive and if you want, it can keep compensating either a joint owner of the policy or any beneficiary you choose for the lifespan of the policy.

Another added benefit, is that for a long time, the scenario was that the rates offered were very insignificant; sometimes as low as 1%-3% and often the interest rates with older traditional annuities which are used to calculate the annuities' payouts were so low. In regards to traditional annuities many claimed that handing over the premium can easily expose you to a good amount of risk of inflation. Due to the current competitive landscape, this is no longer the case.

If you really want to put your savings in an annuity policy, its best to check the prevailing interest rates and it is more likely that now, you'll find the rates are more than competitive given the downside protection and tax deferral index annuities offered.

One perception of indexed annuities is that they are highly illiquid. This could not be further from the truth. Indexed annuities are one of the most liquid assets available on the market, which allows them to now be offered to not only retirees but people of all ages and varying investment time horizons, because annuities offer allowed annual withdrawals of about 10% without any consequences. Couple that flexibility with reducing surrender periods, and it is no wonder these annuity policies are now even offered for those with short-term liquidity needs and for younger demographics.

As a result, if one invests while they are young, he or she may get to use the funds whenever an emergency arises and can be met with the 10% annual allowed withdrawals.

Furthermore, as surrender periods are shortening, you may be allowed to withdraw even more than that.

For a few years now, indexed annuities have granted a secure and protected form of savings for millions of investors on a tax-deferred basis. Indexed annuity policies are the simplest form of annuity policies. They offer most of the benefits given by other annuity policies and guarantee the principal amount along with interest. There are several advantages to considering indexed annuities as a viable investment option.

A lot has changed for the indexed annuity market over the years and very attractive, hard-to-match features have been added to these forms of annuity products, such as an uncapped growth strategy, high participation rates, and competitive spreads, all affixed throughout the duration of the contract.

**CONS**

The benefits and advantages of indexed annuities were discussed at length in the first portion of this chapter, but with advantages also come disadvantages. In recent years, there has been quite a bit of speculation on annuities, specifically indexed annuities, with many investors ruling against them. Annuities have also generated the catch phrase "annuities are not bought, they are sold." We will explore why that perception is so rampant and what the true advantages of indexed annuities are. I hope that you are very excited to do so?

Indexed annuity policies are outwardly rather simple to explain, many indexed products are very complex and complicated to work out. Immense problems come up when trying to settle on which segment of the stock market to index, how much of the market gains should go to an annuity policyholder and the various time frames involved.

- **No dividends**: It is common knowledge that almost 40% of the profits on the S&P 500 index are based on dividends. However, some indexed annuity profits do not include the dividends. Although most policies include dividends given the current competitive landscape, you still need to read the fine print to make sure the dividend policy is or is not part of the return. You have to claim dividends on your taxes annually and index annuities are tax-deferred. As with all open stock market investments, you still have some risk of losing money.

- **Complicated calculation options**: With an indexed annuity, complicated calculations and expressions such as "spread," "cap," "point to point," and "monthly sum" arise. Most agents and insurance companies are not competent in showing you how the calculations actually work. The calculation process is also mentioned above and in the previous chapters as well, and as you can probably tell, it is very complicated.

- **Anniversary date**: With almost all indexed annuity policies, your returns are locked in at the policy's anniversary date. With annuities, policy years are not calculated on a calendar-year basis but from the day the insurance company invests your premium. Again, the interest is only credited to the policy once a year, which is based on the indexed crediting system also discussed above. In addition, once the interest is credited it cannot be taken away during the next year if the calculated index is negative.

- **Surrender charges for certain periods of time**: A good number of the indexed annuity policies sold carry certain surrender period penalties. Although these surrender periods are becoming shorter relative to historical trends, it nonetheless means that the assets are locked up for some period of time, and if touched, you may be penalized. The penalty usually declines per year over the surrender period. Again, you are still allowed to withdraw 10% annually without any penalty. You can always take more money if needed but there is a penalty above the 10% per year annually.

Adding to the complexity, the various indexed annuities offered by different life insurance companies have different ways of calculating the gains. For example, some insurance companies would give you just a certain percentage of the index's overall returns, or set an annual cap and most companies leave out dividends. This is very uncommon in the current indexed annuity market. Therefore, it is highly difficult to accurately calculate how well the annuity in question will perform, using all the different stock market results. With indexed annuity policies that offer no uncapped strategies, which again is quite uncommon these days, they do not at all times match the indexes' full return. As a result they only get a portion of the market's entire return year for the market index it was tied to. As mentioned above, different indexed annuities analyze your gains in different ways.

In annuity policies, the premium/asset paid by the annuitant is taken by the company and is then divided into two parts:

1. The larger share of the money is invested within the company in a stable portfolio of securities, which are guaranteed to grow back to the full amount of premium paid by the end of the policy term.
2. The smaller portion is used to buy call options on the stock index. These call options are a kind of derivative, which will increase considerably in value if the index rises, sometimes more than the actual amount of growth in the index. This profit is then employed to pass along the growth to the annuitants.

This is how insurance companies keep those investments protected from loss, and is widely accepted to be the soundest investment strategy when investing in the stock market: investing in an annuity, while protecting with a hedging strategy.

As discussed in the previous pages, nearly all indexed annuity policies have some sort of annual cap along with, for example, a participation rate. Let's say you invest $100,000 in a seven year indexed annuity policy with a 70% participation rate and a 12% cap. During the first year, the index rises to an enormous 30% for the year. Your total gain would be limited to 12%, since the total gain from the participation rate exceeds this amount (70% of 30% = 21%).

Some policies will keep the gains from one year and reset the caps each year, while others determine the gains made for the term of the policy. The biggest drawback is that if the benchmark rate doesn't increase, you won't get any gains. State laws ensure that indexed policies do provide investors with at least a small amount of guaranteed interest as a form of comfort if the rate does not rise during the period of the annuity policy.

As times have changed for the better, insurance companies are generally offering an indexed annuity product that is very competitive by offering uncapped features within this investment.

The second and third biggest drawbacks concerning annuities are the surrender fees and potential taxes. As discussed earlier, all annuity policies have a surrender period of three to ten years or even longer. Insurance companies set the terms of an annuity this way because the intent and purpose of the annuity is to be used as a long-term retirement money protection vehicle. Not a checking account to pay bills each month.

As discussed, annuity policies come with surrender periods in the event that an early withdrawal is exercised by the annuitant.

Commonly the penalty will be 10% in the early years. If withdrawals are taken from an annuity policy before the owner is aged 59.5 or 60 years, the normal tax rules for qualified accounts impose a 10% penalty on gains made. Early withdrawal penalties are common among nearly any retirement account.

Regular income taxes will also be payable on any gain pulled-out from an annuity. Only a few indexed annuities had a surrender charge spanning longer than 15 years. If you invested in such a policy, but wanted to get out early, the surrender charge could add up to thousands of dollars. This is quite a hefty surcharge for an annuity. The time period becomes insignificant to the asset protection and the account growth, using the index the annuity provides the investor.

The good news is prevailing market forces have led to insurance companies offering some of the best features of an investment product in today's indexed annuities, for which surrender periods are generally shorter and surrender fees usually max out at 10%.

Another drawback associated with indexed annuities used to be the evil games played by the insurance companies. They are the deciding authority behind how much a policy will earn every year. Therefore, they can give you a good deal at first, but change the payout later on. You would be stuck with that annuity and wouldn't be able to get out unless you agree on paying the surrender charge.

Changes to these caveats have been the most advantageous in recent years as all covenants to the indexed annuity policy are thoroughly explained in clear language. Uncapped rates, low spreads and high participation rates are no longer offered as teaser rates, but are fixed for the duration of the policy. Indexed annuity policies are taxed in the same manner as other types of annuities. All the money once invested with the insurance company grows tax-deferred until you take out a distribution.

Once taken out, all distributions are reported and taxed as ordinary income, meaning that every time the company pays you the money, be it monthly, quarterly or yearly, income tax will be deducted on it. In addition, any distribution taken before age 59.5 years is calculated to include an additional 10% early withdrawal penalty. The size of the premium paid into the indexed policy is usually counted as a tax-free return of the principal amount, and is then incorporated with each periodic payment. However, these penalties are applicable only on qualified retirement account plans such as IRAs and 401K plans.

Tax-deferral as discussed is one of the great benefits of buying indexed annuities. Tax-deferral is also lucrative because it allows your money and the interest, to make money and to grow each year uninterrupted without any taxes levied. Although all the gains you make will now be taxed at the normal income tax rate, especially if your earlier means of income were capital gains, you are trading in all the tax privileges of the capital gains tax rate, currently 23.5% at the federal income tax level. The result: you have to pay nearly twice that of your capital gains tax. It is important to note that if you start withdrawing funds at retirement; your income tax rate is likely to be lower, compared to your peak earning years, possibly lower than the capital gains tax rate you may be accustomed to.

Insurance companies are businesses, and the safety and soundness of indexed annuities varies between the different issuers. This is one risk that needs to be addressed. In almost all occasions, though the bare minimum guarantee is based upon a segment of your policy rather than the entire amount. Investors are often warned to be wary of such options. Consider what would happen if their insurer goes bankrupt?

The truth is that even in the stock market, all companies have the possibility of bankruptcy; while it is highly unlikely an insurance company will go bankrupt in the United States. Insurance companies are qualified and approved by the Department of Insurance in the state that they are sold and are re-insured for financial loss of up to $250,000 to $350,000, depending on the state the annuity is sold in.

It is important that the annuity you purchase is from an A-Rated insurance company, which means their financial strength is superior and they are respected in the industry. In 2008, more than 600 banks failed, yet not a single insurance company failed. In 1929, during the Great Depression, nearly 10,000 banks failed and not a single insurance company went under.

Many opponents of indexed annuities also claim they are similar to an IRA, which is basically an individual savings account with tax benefits as explained in the previous chapter. Annuities work with both qualified and non-qualified IRA accounts. Keep in mind that your money is at far more risk in the IRA than if invested in an annuity policy.

IRAs are simply a retirement account where individuals keep investments like stocks, bonds and mutual funds. Either way, an IRA and an indexed annuity policy both help in saving for retirement. Proponents for annuities claim that annuities have no limit on how much money can be invested to attain tax-deferred earnings. The idea behind this tax deferral is that the financial credit value will grow larger in the annuity compared with growth in a comparable taxable investment. However, once you do end up taking out the distributions, they are reported and taxed as ordinary income, as explained above.

Indexed annuities do carry fees. They are not as exorbitant as variable annuities, in which the policy's fees and other costs are potentially very high as they carry a complex combination of commissions, broker fees and transaction fees. Similarly, IRAs also carry low fees, as they are given through your employer; therefore, the costs are reduced when your employer offers you the IRA as part of a benefits package.

The bottom line is that if you decide to purchase an annuity policy, you need to avoid getting trapped within the cons, especially variable annuity products, which are seldom useful for investors but always lucrative for the seller, as you can see from the commission rates, the surrender periods and penalties accompanied by variable annuities.

# CHAPTER FOUR
## Behind the Curtain – The Insider View on Fixed Annuities

An expert in business matters compared the indexed annuity policy with the original "Wizard of Oz" film. According to him, when Dorothy and her friends went to see the Wizard of Oz, they were in awe until Toto the dog pulled the curtain back to reveal that the wizard was just a man running a soundboard system, nothing fancy or commendable. You may want to compare that scene to indexed annuities. But relax—we're not talking about variable annuities. We're talking about fixed indexed annuities. A sound fundamental retirement investment.

After going through the comprehensive discussion on the pros and cons of indexed annuities, you might be asking: Where do these annuities fit? What exactly are these alleged win-win investments? Who's most likely to benefit by purchasing them?

Annuity policies are best for income riders and for income planning because annuities are actually retirement saving resources. But with all the changes undergone by the indexed annuity market in the past decade, more people are using annuities as an alternative for mutual funds because they participate in the stock market and offer 100% protection. Many indexed annuity policies also offer a penalty-free sum which can be withdrawn every year. For example, the right to extract 10% of the annuity's value every year is a powerful tool you can use to leverage gains and earnings in your golden years of retirement.

You should understand by now, as a business expert has rightly put it, that, "the upside to an indexed annuity is that there is no downside." The downside is very limited, and happens only with a variable index annuity, which has higher fees and no principal guarantee while offering no guaranteed growth rate on the account. It should be clear by now that indexed annuities provide a great investment strategy, no matter what your disposition. Even if you don't have any financial reserves, the fact that you can annually withdraw 10% of the policy without penalty offers a great backup plan.

**Now, the most critical question: Are indexed annuities too good to be true?** *The answer is obviously NO.*

Fixed index annuities give you asset protection with the upside growth potential of an index working in the stock market.

That's even considering the complex workings of the annuities along with the personal experience of every individual who has acquired indexed annuities by now.

The Financial Industry Regulatory Authority (FINRA), also the largest non-governmental watchdog for securities firms doing business within the U.S., issued an alert back in 2010, noting that the products are "anything but easy to understand." And thus you can lose money, in spite of all the sales offers made to the contrary. FINRA's vice president also believes that when investing in annuities, especially indexed annuities, people need to be concerned with the three most pressing issues related to indexed annuities: the complexity, cost and liquidity.

FINRA has raised subsequent cautions about indexed annuity policies.

- **Rate of interest**: Insurers generally use a combination of indexing choices, which include: participation rates, spreads, margins, asset charges and interest rate caps, to calculate the profits on the indexed part of the annuity policy. To further confuse matters, many indexed annuity policies also permit the insurer to alter these calculation methods, either yearly or at the beginning of the next policy tenure. This makes it that much more important to make sure you have an expert in this area in your corner.

- **Indexing process**: Ask your insurer about the process the company will use to credit interest to your annuity, as well as if and how it works with the indexing options and choices above. This can have a considerable effect on your annuity income. Again, it is vital to speak with a retirement specialist who is an expert in this area before making any investments.

- **Omission of dividends**: Some indexed annuities count the profits made just from the changes in the market price on the index, and do not include dividends. However, one must still read the fine print to confirm that the total return, inclusive of dividends, is what is used to assess profits.

- **Losing money with indexed annuities**: Companies normally only owe 87.5% of the paid premium, but this is only applied when you cancel everything right at the beginning. If you go on about fulfilling the contract it should not have an impact.

- **There is limited liquidity**: Since annuity policies are a time-sensitive investment option, for a certain period your funds are locked from full withdrawal, other than the annual allowed amount of 10%. Remember there are certain rules about surrender charges and surrender periods, usually 10% and

10 years, respectively, after which such charges are ZERO.

One needs to be hyper-vigilant when getting an indexed annuity, because something that benefits someone else may not benefit you and you cannot compare their indexed annuity policy to the one you're about to acquire.

Moving on, we look at the different viewpoints and perspectives of those who know the inside scoop on indexed annuities.

- **Mike Volner** (Volner Financial Group): Mr. Volner has sold health and life insurance practically all his life. Lately though, he has shifted his focus to annuities. Stating he has learned that annuities can be a robust financial foundation, especially if you want your money to sit and grow for you or if you need income that is guaranteed throughout retirement.

- **Jim Brogan** (Founder and President of Brogan Financial): Mr. Brogan states that people mostly want safety and security for their finances. However, they don't want to sacrifice growth potential. Annuities can be very powerful tools to generate growth potential if used correctly.

- **John Zidan** (Owner and President, Retirement First): Mr. Zidan claims he overcame the fear of surrender charges by telling himself that there is a price for liquidity. He then asks a question: "would you rather have 50 percent gains and no losses or 100 percent gains and 100 percent losses?" He answers this by the "Power of Zero."

  Therefore, even if the market crashes, your investments stay unchanged and when the market rises, they increase, without having to start from a loss and then work their way up.

- **Mark Pruitt** (CEO, President and Founder of Strategic Estate Planning Services Inc.): After working with clients for two years via conducting various workshops, Mr. Pruitt came to the conclusion that people want safety, growth, zero or fewer taxes and 100% liquidity at all times. However, he says that such a product doesn't exist. According to him, most people are willing to give up some liquidity for safety and growth. One solution could be an income annuity.

- **Jeff Bucher** (President and Co-Founder, Citizen Advisory Group): For Mr. Bucher, it's all about taking control. "With less at risk, they will lose less money. They can take control rather than being fearful... We can show [clients] that they can take control, turn off all the noise, and build their own pension and an income stream that won't run out before they run out of breath. And they can give money to the kids."

- **Jack Keeter** (President of Jack Keeter & Associates and the Jack Keeter Study Group): "People don't need an annuity; they need good advice." He talks about how important it is to develop a bond or trust with your advisor; any advisor loyal to you would never tell you to get an annuity if you don't need one, and not everyone needs an annuity.

- **Tim Maurer** (Certified Financial Planner and Vice President of the Financial

Consulate in Hunt Valley): Mr. Maurer advises people to hunt for any low or no commission annuity that has very little or no surrender charge. This will eliminate some of the unfavorable features of annuities.

- **Douglas Dubitsky** (Vice President, Product Management and Development for Retirement Solutions, Guardian Life Insurance Co. of America): For Mr. Dubitsky, it's about the correct advice given to people on an individual basis. Again not everyone requires an annuity. Advisors need to help people understand on a personal level how to mitigate the risks they face during retirement and how best to control the assets they've been accumulating.

- **Dan Solin** (author of "The Smartest Retirement Book You'll Ever Read"): According to Mr. Solin, it is best to consider using numerous insurance companies to diversify your risk when investing in indexed annuities. In addition, buying immediate annuities at different stages might be helpful for you.

Another indexed annuity executive wanted to reveal some kept back and hidden industry secrets to consumers and equip them with some significant truths and facts about indexed annuities. Fearing an industry reaction, he remained anonymous.

- **How indexes are selected, crafted and manipulated?** This is the executive's number one apprehension about annuities. He states that when an indexed annuity policy is designed, the company has to make sure they also get a return on the investment.

Therefore, the policy is manipulated and crafted in such a way that the functions of the policy attain the desired profit. If you have a look at lottery payments or game show prizes, you might notice how the winners are rarely paid lump sum but always annuitized over several years. Why is that? The main reason is that underwriters know they can earn interest on the annuity and get back some of the money they are giving away to you as a prize, be it Lotto or "Let's Make A Deal."

- **Why do a majority of the indexed annuities have surrender charges for more than 10 years? This is no longer the case.** Historically, extended surrender charge periods led to higher commissions awarded to the agent, those products were marketed the most. However, with an open market of competitive products that consumers find most beneficial, indexed annuities have been revolutionized in many fronts. One of those is reduction of surrender periods.

  o **Index options and renewal rates:** Another relic of the past is that nearly all index choices are set for the preliminary deal of the policy and not for the whole term. Therefore, if the cap is 6% during the first year, typically the renewal rates persist declining over the lifetime of the policy. Until recently many companies did not offer reasonable renewal rates. But, the evolution of indexed annuities has changed that. Today retirement specialists can provide investment vehicles that offer, guaranteed interest rates, that are signed into

the contract to be effective
throughout the duration of the
policy.

o **Hedge fund or private equity
companies buying index annuity
carriers:** Hedge funds coming into
the industry have definitely
changed things. Hedge fund
agents want a much higher return
than a traditional insurance
company selling an annuity. They
are positive they can administer
the money better to create a higher
rate of return via their proprietary
investment formulas.

An annuity is like a sanctuary for an
individual's money where the money can also
grow. The only change of path that annuities
have is upward and every year you will collect
a specific amount of interest. Therefore, you
no longer have to fret about risking your
retirement savings in an IRA or 401K. That is
why throughout this book our goal has been
for you to learn about fixed index annuities,
how they protect your money and how we can
help you in purchasing the right type of
annuity that meets your financial and

retirement needs.

This book, **"The Pros & Cons of Index Annuities,"** is essentially all about the advice. Not everyone will require buying an annuity, but it is becoming a suitable investment option for a growing number of investors, not only as a retirement tax-deferred pension and investment vehicle but also for younger investors seeking alternative forms of retirement saving beyond the standard IRA and 401K.

Hopefully, you have not only learned the basics of what index annuities are and how they work, but you've also learned why they are so important.

The indexed annuity world will continue to grow at a much faster rate, especially with all the transformation the industry has experienced the last few years. If index annuities seem right for you and your needs and what you have learned so far in this book resonates with you, we invite you to continue the conversation with us and schedule a discovery session.

**http://www.ProsAndConsOfAnnuities.com/discovery**

# Conclusion

Indexed annuity policies are the hottest and the most over-endorsed products within the annuity and insurance world. Furthermore, the "too good to be true" return scenarios being pitched and offered to some customers are helping insurance companies transform the pitched ideas into record sales. There are more than $250 billion in annuities sold each year and growing with the number of retirees that are finding an annuity the right fit as they turn 65 and older.

An indexed annuity policy is considered the reverse side of a life insurance policy, which allows the annuity to pay you while you're still alive. One of the nicest things about an annuity policy is that not only are your gains protected while participating in the stock market but your annuity can be structured to create an income for you and your spouse no matter how long you live. The annuity will pay your beneficiary the unused portion after you die. A 401K or IRA cannot offer that type of guarantee.

Indexed annuity policies aim to provide income during your retirement years, either in the form of a lump sum or as regular payments, for a particular period of time or over your entire life, while also allowing withdrawals of up to 10% each year without penalty. Payments could be monthly, quarterly or yearly when you receive your disbursements. The income you receive can be immediate or deferred and you can choose to receive it in fixed or variable amounts.

This largely depends on the type of option selected with your indexed annuity policy. Taxes are deferred until you start receiving income, and payments continue to the spouse and then beneficiaries when the husband and wife are gone for the length of the contract.

In addition, you can also have a joint owner with yourself on a non-qualified policy. It used to be that such products were not always as easy and simple as they sounded, like insurance products, which were easier to explain on paper than in real life. Since indexed annuity policies have evolved, most of the covenants are pretty straightforward and are now well explained. Having read this book you should congratulate yourself on taking action and making the right decisions today that can help you change your life and the landscape of your retirement, for your legacy and beyond, starting right now. If you are ready to make the discovery, visit:

**http://www.ProsAndConsOfAnnuities.com/discovery**

The most complex and intricate instrument, (the stock market) has been replaced with a simple and straightforward index annuity or fixed index annuity policy.

When you visit the Discovery page at the link above please complete the short Discovery form. This brief form is all that we will need in order to assign you a Retirement Assessment Coordinator and to schedule your one-on-one **Retirement Assessment Discovery session**.

Our goal is to provide you Independent information so you can make the best choice for yourself. If you opt not to use us that is okay, we just want what is best for you.

We warn you to be careful of advisors who don't have your best interest in mind when it comes to certain annuities products. For example, avoid any loss in times of uncertain market performance. When working with our Retirement Legacy Specialist, we will show you exactly how to avoid financial missteps and vulnerability, as well as hidden costs. Frankly, without our guidance, you may find yourself signing up for unfavorable terms or the riskier types of variable annuities. We want to help you avoid those mistakes.

In our view indexed annuities are the most secure investment vehicle that you can have in your retirement portfolio. Often an annuity investment will be a fit for one person, but may not fit you in the same way. It really depends on your circumstances and your time perspective.

If it is a fit, our goal is to help you succeed using annuities as a measure of protection on the savings in your retirement portfolio. The point being made here is not whether an indexed annuity is a good or a bad product. As advisors we help people understand on a personal level how to mitigate the risks they face during retirement. We can show you how best to control the assets they've been accumulating and avoid running out of money before you die.

Index annuities have granted a secure and protected form of saving for millions of investors and many of our clients on a tax-deferred basis. An investment strategy using annuities can be a robust financial foundation, especially if you want your money to be protected from risk and grow for the income needed in retirement using an index to see significant growth in retirement.

The best part about indexed annuities are that even if the market were to crash, the initial amount that you invest (the principal) stays completely unchanged and when the market rises your index annuity policy increases without having to start from zero.

It pays to have the annuity policy working for you to increase your income at a reasonable rate for return. Your annuity policy keeps your principal intact and your gains are locked in each and every year. So technically, you never lose money and the policy ensures you end up saving.

In extremely rare instances insurance companies can fail, like any business and go bankrupt. Therefore, it is very important that you check the financial strength of the company offering you the annuity before you end up buying the annuity from them. I always recommend big, strong and safe companies with an "A" rating to our clients.

Now that you have a much better understanding of what an index annuity is and what it can do for your retirement portfolio you can consult with my firm at Lucas Insurance Services Inc. to find out which annuity policy may work best for your retirement needs.

The devil is in the details as you have learned by reading this book. We're happy to continue the conversation and offer a personal Discovery session for you.

Visit our website:
**http://www.ProsAndConsOfAnnuities.com/discovery**

Fill out the brief form on the page for your one-on-one retirement Discovery session.

## About the Author

I am a licensed insurance agent and retirement planning specialist with more than 30 years of experience. I have studied, investigated and educated myself to uncover the facts about all annuities. Now I am able to provide you with those facts - both positive and negative - to help you make the best decision for yourself.

You could have numerous retirement investment objectives. They might include saving for a certain goal, leaving your loved ones on a secure footing once you are gone, or generating a lifelong income stream. Unfortunately, it is harder than ever to achieve those objectives, with ever-growing demand and limited sources for finding a solution. Today's economy makes it harder to save for retirement and most people are living paycheck to paycheck. College today costs as much as some people make in a year or more, while a 529 college savings plan can cause problems for other forms of financial aid. Many companies do not have traditional pensions, but instead offer 401K and IRAs, which have limitations on how much you can invest in them each year. Now, more than ever, it is the individual's responsibility to establish and invest wisely to build a financially secure future.

If you are anything like I am, you want as much information as possible about anything you are looking at using, buying or in any way making a big decision about. If you are reading this book, that is precisely what you are doing. To prepare for writing "The Pros and Cons of Index Annuities," I investigated and studied all types of annuities to uncover the secrets. Now I can pass this information onto you, so you'll also have the knowledge of an expert.

I believe I had the same questions you have, starting with, *"What are the pros and cons of index annuities?"*

Lindahl Lucas

Made in the USA
Lexington, KY
12 January 2019